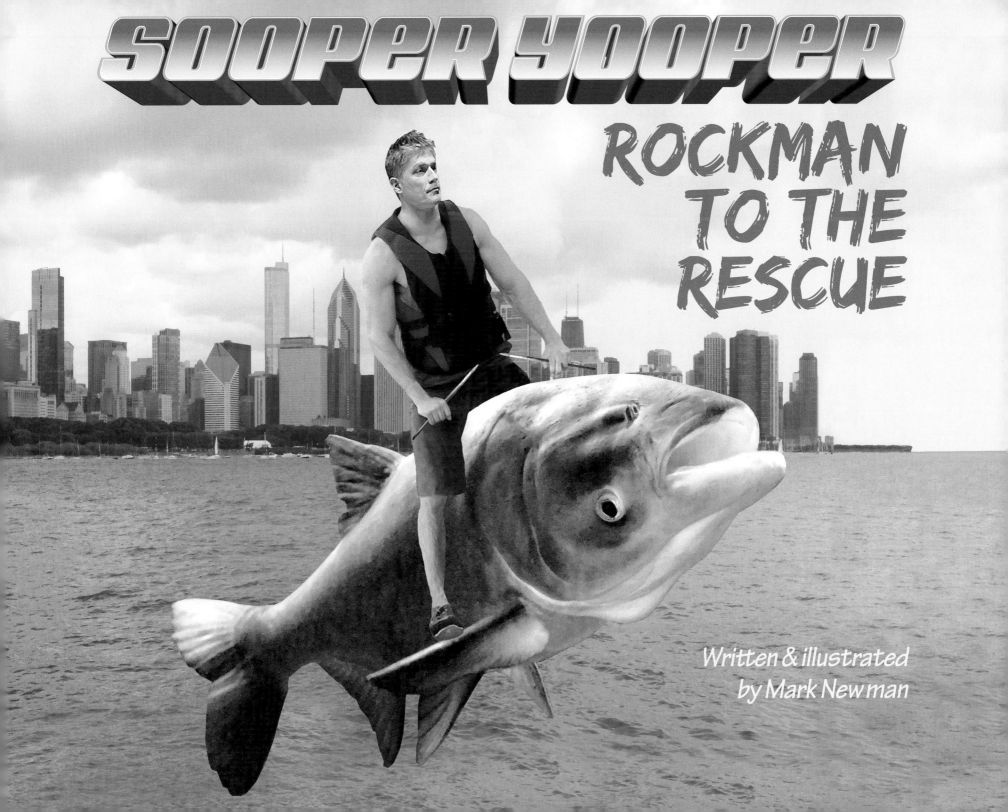

Sooper Yooper: Rockman to the Rescue is published in conjunction with the exhibition,
Alexis Rockman: The Great Lakes Cycle
COPYRIGHT © 2018 Mark Newman
Artworks © Alexis Rockman

Alexis Rockman: The Great Lakes Cycle is made possible through the generosity of the following sponsors:

Wege Foundation
Frey Foundation
Eenhoorn, LLC
Kendall College of Art and Design
James and Mary Nelson
Blue Water Communications
Greg and Meg Willit
Diana Dopson/D*Lux Travel
Bill Scarbrough and Kate Kesteloot Scarbrough

National Endowment for the Arts
LaFontsee Galleries and Framing
Ferris State University
Wolverine Worldwide Foundation
Cascade Engineering
Dirk and June Hoffius
Robert Daverman, AIA / Grand Rapids Community Foundation
Prime, Buchholz & Associates, Inc.
J. Visser Design
(Donor list as of October 30, 2017)

Additional funding is provided by the GRAM Exhibition Society.

Alexis Rockman: The Great Lakes Cycle Exhibition Itinerary

January 28–April 29, 2018	Grand Rapids Art Museum
June 2–October 1, 2018	Chicago Cultural Center
October 19, 2018–January 27, 2019	Museum of Contemporary Art, Cleveland
October 5, 2019–January 5, 2020	Weisman Art Museum, University of Minnesota, Minneapolis
May 9–August 16, 2020	Flint Institute of Arts

PUBLISHED BY THE GRAND RAPIDS ART MUSEUM
101 Monroe Center NW, Grand Rapids, Michigan 49503 www.artmuseumgr.org
ISBN: 978-0-942159-35-6 (hardcover)

Thanks to Alexis Rockman, Dana Friis-Hansen, Jolie Masters, Christopher Bruce, Jon Carfagno, Mark Van Putten and Jill Leonard as well as those whose images appear in the book: Lisa Newman, Rodney Pierson, Monica Phillips, Andy and Karla Schmidt, Paul VanDyke, Patrick Werner and Jerry Ziomkowski, along with Jennifer Gabrys and her kids Mariella, Nicholas and Evan. Special thanks to Kathy Newman for her editing and suggestions.

SOOPER YOOPER
ROCKMAN TO THE RESCUE

Written & illustrated by Mark Newman

Inspired by the life and work of artist Alexis Rockman

This hardcover edition was produced by Original Smith Printing,
a member of the Forest Stewardship Council (FSC),
dedicated to conserving rainforests and recycling all excess paper.

To Gabriella,

Mark Newman

"Guard the Great Lakes!"

FSC
www.fsc.org

MIX
Paper from
responsible sources
FSC® C021826

For more information, visit www.SooperYooper.com

Watching the Great Lakes kept Billy Cooper on guard.
As Sooper Yooper, it had become his calling card.
Protecting water and land, he continually starred.
But halting invaders was increasingly hard.

With the arrival of rock snot, things got even worse.
Whether swimming or fishing, it was a real curse.
Then toxic algae appeared, adding an Erie verse.
Pretty soon, the Great Lakes might need a hearse.

Cooper wrote to his friend Rockman, an artist of might,
Whose passion for the planet was certainly not trite.
Rockman, he knew, could draw attention to the lakes' plight
Before the mercury reached numbers untold in Fahrenheit.

Rockman was from New York City, one of the world's great places.
Prolific in painting, his work filled countless art spaces.
Water was frequently his subject, climate change often its basis,
He pursued evidence like an attorney on criminal cases.

From an early age, Rockman was taught to exercise his mind.
Catching frogs and turtles was how he was most inclined.
He also liked bats, rats and other creatures who are often maligned.
Truth be told, he might have preferred animals over humankind.

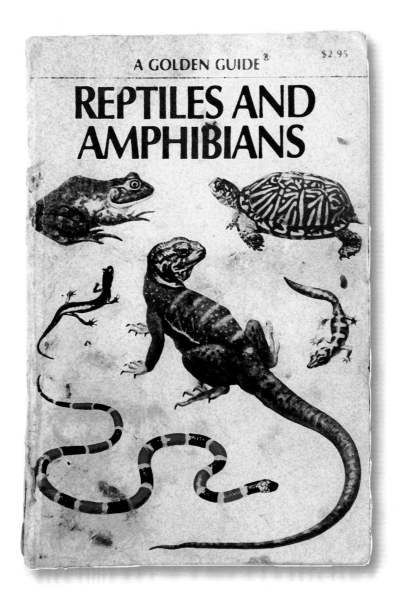

Rockman was fascinated by science; he loved to read,
Golden Field Guides and magazines filled his need.
Amphibians, reptiles, birds and even the centipede
Captured his imagination, like monster movies indeed!

Many days were spent at Turtle Pond in the Central Park air.
Where he spent hour upon hour in the bright sun's glare.
Watching fish jump and birds swim was a regular affair.
So much to do there, boredom never had a prayer.

Across the street was a natural history museum.
The dioramas were so amazing, you just had to see 'em.

As a budding artist, he was drawn to smaller displays, too.
Fascinated by their creativity, color and hue.
Every detail captured his view.
Every fact sticking to him like glue.

For Rockman, every project was an adventure, a discovery-bent feat.
From Guyana to Costa Rica, he ventured far from Main Street
To witness flora and fauna not found in any hotel suite.
With the stamina of an athlete, his missions went beyond concrete.

Like a rolling stone, Rockman gathered no moss.
In the frigid waters of Antarctica, he was his own boss.

Wherever he journeyed, he went without hype.
In the company of seals, who could gripe?

Over the years, Rockman has traveled all over the world.
He's been to so many places, his toes should be curled.
At home, it was around his rescue dog Padme that his life swirled.
Now the Great Lakes beckoned; new discoveries to be unfurled.

Like Cooper, Rockman knew you should know what you're talking about.
The more facts you have, the less there is to doubt.
To best study the Great Lakes, Rockman planned out his route.
In the process, he'd eat lots of Coneys, pasties and 'kraut.

Rockman visited Jill, a fish biologist and real scholar.
The students in her lab make good use of every dollar.
From lamprey to sturgeon and round goby much smaller,
She shared any and all knowledge worth a holler.

In Minnesota, Rockman went to another museum of natural history, gathering up all the clues he might need to solve a perplexing mystery.

His journey offered sights upon which to dwell,
From Niagara Falls and its heavy swell
To Pictured Rocks and its colorful carousel.
There was nary a vision that didn't cast a spell.

Rockman ended his trip the way he began it.

Realizing that he cannot take anything for "granite."

His position now rock solid, like stannite.*

His mission still was to save the planet.

*a mineral made of copper, iron and tin.

Encouragement came from Dana, a man with an eye that was keen.
He knew Rockman from his previous work on the artistic scene.
Living in the Midwest, he knew the value of keeping the Great Lakes clean.
With Sooper Yooper and Rockman together, they might keep them pristine.

As director of an art museum that was green[*],
Dana had the perfect platform for an artist's widescreen.
Carpets from recycled plastic, water culled from rain – hardly routine,
With natural light, it was the most efficient ever seen.

*GRAM is the world's first LEED® Gold Certified art museum.

"Time is of the essence with Asian carp at the door,"
Billy Cooper told Rockman from the front lines of the war.
Onward to Chicago where these invaders were poised to soar.
"Unless we get politicians to stop 'em, there will be more."

Rockman headed back to New York, his research complete.
He would paint five vast murals, an ambitious feat.
One for each lake, but with a theme more discreet.
They would take time, but when finished, would be rather sweet.

Rockman approached his painting with extraordinary zeal,
Layering ideas to support his ecological spiel.
Above and below were many creatures, from eagle to elk and even an eel.
So much to view - you could never see 'em all in an automobile.

Dana appreciated that Rockman provided his paintings with a key,
Creating a graphical silhouette of everything the viewer could see.

KEY TO TROPICAL MIGRANTS PAINTING

His works made a strong impression, filling viewers with awe,
A variety of life forms that fit together like a giant jigsaw.

People captured Rockman's paintings to share with their friends.
Powerful images to stir and stoke passions from their own lens.

And if they recoiled at monsters found in the abyss.
They responded en masse to fix what was amiss.

Young and old alike rallied to the cause and paraded with signs.
Water, it was clear, is to humans like ketchup is to Heinz.

Inspired by Rockman's message, concerned citizens drew up a petition.
For many, guarding the Great Lakes was becoming their mission.

Familes joined forces to fight all types of pollution.
Not wanting to be the problem, they became the solution.

With visions of giant carp still dancing in his head,
Rockman was happy to put his pet project to bed.
While word of his Great Lakes paintings continued to spread,
Politicians were taking notice of all that was said.

THE DAILY NEWS

www.dailynews.com — THE WORLD'S FAVORITE NEWSPAPER — · Since 1879

ROCKMAN TO THE RESCUE

43

For Billy Cooper, Rockman had arrrived like a jewel.
Coming to the rescue with his brush as his tool.
But he still needed to be like a lifeguard at the pool.
Always protecting the Great Lakes, stubborn as a mule.